CHRISTOPHER MORRIS

A Beginner's Guide to
Understanding AI

First edition

Contents

1 Chapter 1: Introduction to Artificial Intelligence

Understanding the Concept of Artificial Intelligence

Artificial Intelligence (AI) is a ground-breaking field that has revolutionized various aspects of human life. It encompasses the development and implementation of intelligent machines that can perform tasks that typically require human intelligence. The tasks include speech recognition, problem-solving, learning, planning, and decision-making. The concept of AI aims to create machines that can mimic and replicate human cognitive abilities, leading to remarkable advancements in technology and society.

Brief History of AI

The journey of artificial intelligence dates back to ancient times when humans first attempted to create intelligent machines. The idea of artificial beings has been present in mythology, folklore, and literature, captivating human imagination for centuries. However, it was not until the 20th century that significant progress was made.

In 1956, the Dartmouth Conference marked the birth of AI as an official field of study. At this conference, leading scientists and researchers gathered to develop machines that could showcase intelligence. The term "artificial intelligence" itself was coined during this event.

During the early years of AI research, the focus was primarily on building systems that could solve complex mathematical problems and perform logical reasoning. Symbolic AI, also known as Good Old-Fashioned AI (GOFAI), uses symbolic logic as a basis for representing knowledge and manipulating it. This approach laid the foundation for future developments in the field.

However, progress in AI faced significant challenges and setbacks. The initial optimism surrounding the field led to unrealistic expectations, often referred to as the "AI winter." Funding and interest dwindled, and it seemed as though AI research had hit a dead end. Yet, the field experienced resurgences in the 1980s and 1990s, with advancements in machine learning and the rise of expert systems.

In recent years, breakthroughs in AI have been fuelled by the availability of vast amounts of data, increased computing power, and advancements in algorithms. Machine learning, deep learning, and neural networks have become prominent fields of AI, enabling the development of intelligent systems that can perceive, understand, and learn from data.

CHAPTER 1: INTRODUCTION TO ARTIFICIAL INTELLIGENCE

Importance and Relevance of AI in Today's World

Artificial intelligence has become a driving force behind transformative changes in various domains. Its importance and relevance in today's world cannot be overstated. Here are a few key areas where AI has made a significant impact:

Healthcare: AI has the potential to revolutionize healthcare by improving diagnostics, personalized medicine, and drug discovery. Intelligent systems can analyze medical records, and detect patterns, and assist doctors in making accurate diagnoses. AI-powered robots can also perform complex surgeries with unparalleled precision.

Transportation: Self-driving cars and autonomous vehicles are becoming a reality, thanks to AI. These technologies have the potential to enhance road safety, reduce traffic congestion, and provide mobility solutions for the elderly and disabled.

Finance: AI algorithms are used in various financial applications, such as fraud detection, algorithmic trading, and credit scoring. These intelligent systems can analyze vast amounts of financial data, identify suspicious patterns, and make informed recommendations.

Manufacturing: AI-powered robots and automation have transformed the manufacturing industry, leading to increased efficiency, precision, and productivity. Intelligent systems can handle complex tasks, adapt to changes in the production line, and optimize resource allocation.

Education: AI has the potential to revolutionize education by personalizing learning experiences, providing individualized feedback, and automating administrative tasks. Intelligent tutoring systems can adapt to students' needs, ensuring effective and engaging learning.

Customer Service: Chatbots and virtual assistants powered by AI have become increasingly prevalent in customer service. These intelligent systems can understand and respond to customer queries, improving response times and enhancing user experiences.

These examples merely scratch the surface of the immense potential AI holds for transforming numerous other fields, including agriculture, energy, cybersecurity, and entertainment. Conclusion

As we embark on this journey through the fascinating world of artificial intelligence, it is crucial to grasp the concept, understand its historical context, and appreciate its significance in today's world. AI has the power to redefine the way we live, work, and interact with technology. With each passing day, breakthroughs and advancements in AI are shaping our future, promising a world where intelligent machines collaborate with humans to solve complex challenges and create unimaginable possibilities. So, let us dive deeper into the realm of artificial intelligence and explore its incredible potential.

2 Chapter 2: The Fundamentals of AI

Exploring the building blocks of AI

Artificial Intelligence (AI) has become a ubiquitous term in today's technology-driven world. From virtual personal assistants to autonomous vehicles, AI has revolutionized various industries. However, to truly understand AI, it is essential to grasp its fundamental building blocks.

At its core, AI refers to the development of computer systems that can perform tasks that typically require human intelligence. These tasks include perception, learning, reasoning, problem-solving, and decision-making. To achieve these capabilities, AI relies on a combination of different technologies and approaches.

Differentiating between narrow AI and general AI

Narrow AI, also known as weak AI, refers to AI systems designed to perform specific tasks with a high degree of proficiency.

These systems are built to excel in a single domain and cannot generalize knowledge to other areas. Examples of narrow AI include speech recognition, image classification, and virtual personal assistants like Siri or Alexa.

On the other hand, general AI, also known as strong AI or artificial general intelligence (AGI), aims to replicate the broad range of human cognitive abilities. General AI systems possess the capacity to understand, learn, and apply knowledge across multiple domains. While we have made significant advancements in narrow AI, achieving true general AI remains a formidable challenge.

Overview of machine learning and deep learning

Machine learning is a subset of AI that enables systems to automatically learn and improve from experience without being explicitly programmed. It relies on algorithms that analyze data, identify patterns, and make predictions or decisions based on those patterns. Machine learning can be broadly categorized into three types: supervised learning, unsupervised learning, and reinforcement learning.

Supervised learning involves training a model on labeled data, where the desired output is known. The model learns to make predictions by finding relationships between the inputs and outputs. This approach is commonly used in tasks like image recognition or spam detection.

Unsupervised learning, on the other hand, deals with unlabelled data, where the model must discover patterns or structures on

its own. This type of learning is often used for tasks such as clustering, anomaly detection, or recommendation systems.

Reinforcement learning involves training an agent to interact with an environment and learn from the feedback it receives. The agent aims to maximize a reward signal while navigating through a sequence of actions. Reinforcement learning has found success in applications such as game playing and robotics.

Deep learning is a subset of machine learning that focuses on artificial neural networks inspired by the structure and function of the human brain. Deep learning algorithms, known as deep neural networks, use multiple layers of interconnected artificial neurons to process and learn from vast amounts of data. This approach has achieved remarkable results in image and speech recognition, natural language processing, and even autonomous driving.

The power of deep learning lies in its ability to automatically extract complex features and representations from raw data. By leveraging large-scale datasets and powerful computational resources, deep neural networks can uncover intricate patterns that were previously beyond the reach of traditional machine learning algorithms.

Future possibilities and considerations

As AI continues to advance, it holds tremendous potential to transform various industries and change the way we live and work. However, with such transformative power comes a range of considerations and challenges.

Ethics and responsible AI development are of paramount importance. Ensuring that AI systems are fair, transparent, and accountable is crucial to prevent biases or unintended consequences. It is essential to establish ethical guidelines and regulations to guide the development and deployment of AI technologies.

Moreover, the societal impact of AI cannot be overlooked. As

AI automates various tasks, it has the potential to reshape job markets and societal structures. Preparing for these changes through education and re-skilling programs will be essential to mitigate any negative consequences and create a balanced AI-powered future.

In conclusion, understanding the fundamentals of AI is crucial for navigating the evolving landscape of this transformative technology. By exploring the building blocks of AI, differentiating between narrow and general AI, and gaining an overview of machine learning and deep learning, the foundation for further exploration into more advanced concepts and applications of AI. As AI continues to push the boundaries of human ingenuity, we must approach its development and deployment with careful consideration and responsible decision-making.

3 Chapter 3: AI Applications in Everyday Life

Introduction

Artificial Intelligence (AI) has made significant advancements in recent years, revolutionizing various industries and transforming the way we live. This chapter delves into the integration of AI into our daily activities, highlighting its applications in virtual assistants, smart devices, autonomous vehicles, healthcare, finance, and entertainment industries.

AI in Virtual Assistants, Smart Devices, and Autonomous Vehicles

Virtual Assistants Virtual assistants have become omnipresent in our lives, helping us with tasks and enhancing our productivity. Powered by AI, these assistants understand natural language and provide personalized responses.

They can schedule appointments, answer questions, play music, and even control other smart devices in our homes. Companies such as Amazon with Alexa, Apple with Siri, and Google with Google Assistant have integrated AI into their virtual assistants, making them increasingly intelligent and intuitive.

Smart Devices AI has brought a new era of connectivity and automation to our homes through smart devices. From smart speakers to smart thermostats and smart lights, these devices utilize AI algorithms to learn our preferences and adapt to our needs. For instance, AI-powered thermostats can learn our temperature preferences and adjust the heating or cooling accordingly, leading to energy efficiency and cost savings. The integration of AI into smart devices makes our lives more convenient, comfortable, and efficient.

Autonomous Vehicles One of the most prominent applications of AI can be seen in the rise of autonomous vehicles. These vehicles leverage AI algorithms to perceive their surroundings, make decisions, and navigate without human intervention. AI enables them to analyze vast amounts of data from sensors, cameras, and radars, ensuring safe and efficient transportation. Autonomous vehicles have the potential to reduce accidents, traffic congestion, and fuel consumption, revolutionizing the way we commute.

AI in Healthcare, Finance, and Entertainment Industries

Healthcare AI has made significant strides in the healthcare industry, revolutionizing diagnostics, treatment, and patient care. Machine learning algorithms can analyze medical images such as X-rays and MRIs, aiding in the detection of diseases like cancer at an early stage. AI-powered chatbots provide real-time medical advice, reducing the burden on healthcare providers and enhancing accessibility. Moreover, AI enables the analysis of massive patient data, leading to improved precision medicine and personalized treatment plans.

Finance AI has transformed the finance industry, enabling faster and more accurate decision-making. AI algorithms can analyze vast amounts of financial data, detect patterns, and predict market trends. This helps financial institutions in fraud detection, risk assessment, and investment recommendations. AI-powered chatbots also assist customers with financial queries and transactions, providing personalized and efficient services. The integration of AI in finance enhances efficiency, security, and customer satisfaction.

Entertainment AI has revolutionized the entertainment industry, enhancing content creation, recommendation systems, and immersive experiences. Streaming platforms like Netflix and Spotify use AI algorithms to analyze user preferences and behavior, providing personalized recommendations. AI-driven content creation tools automate tasks such as video editing and music composition, enabling creative professionals to focus on the artistic aspects. Virtual reality and augmented reality technologies powered by AI provide immersive gaming experiences and interactive storytelling.

Conclusion

The integration of AI into our daily lives has transformed the way we interact with technology and conduct our activities.
From virtual assistants and smart devices to autonomous vehicles, AI has made our lives more convenient, efficient, and connected. Moreover, AI's applications in healthcare, finance, and entertainment industries have revolutionized the way we receive medical care, manage finances, and

consume content. As AI continues to evolve, it will undoubtedly lead to further advancements and improvements in our everyday lives.

4 Chapter 4: AI in Industry and Business

Introduction:

Artificial Intelligence (AI) has emerged as a transformative force in various sectors and industries. Its ability to mimic human intelligence, learn from vast amounts of data, and perform complex tasks has revolutionized the way businesses operate. In this chapter, we will explore the impact of AI on different sectors and industries, focusing on its applications in manufacturing, logistics, customer service, data analysis, and decision-making processes.

Impact of AI on Different Sectors and Industries:

Manufacturing: AI has revolutionized the manufacturing sector by optimizing processes, enhancing productivity, and improving product quality. Smart manufacturing systems powered by AI can detect anomalies in real-time, leading to faster and moreaccuratequalitycontrol. AI-enabled robots and automated systems can handle repetitive tasks with precision, reducing human error and increasing efficiency. Furthermore, predictive maintenance powered by AI algorithms can identify potential equipment failures before they occur, minimizing downtime and maximizing productivity.

Logistics: AI has transformed the logistics industry, making supply chain management more efficient and cost-effective. Intelligent algorithms can analyze vast amounts of data, such as historical shipping patterns, weather conditions, and real-time traffic updates, to optimize delivery routes and minimize transportation costs. AI-powered predictive analytics can also forecast demand accurately, enabling businesses to optimize inventory levels and reduce storage and carrying costs.

Customer Service: AI has revolutionized customer service by providing personalized and efficient support. Virtual assistants, chatbots, and voice recognition systems powered by AI can handle customer inquiries, provide instant responses, and assist with troubleshooting. Natural Language Processing (NLP) algorithms enable these AI systems to understand and respond to customers in real time, leading to improved customer satisfaction and reduced response times. Additionally, sentiment analysis algorithms can assess customer feedback and sentiment, providing valuable insights for businesses to enhance their products and services.

AI in Data Analysis and Decision-Making Processes:

Data Analysis: The exponential growth of data generated by businesses has led to a need for advanced analytics tools. AIpowered data analysis techniques can process vast amounts

of structured and unstructured data, identify patterns, and extract meaningful insights. Machine Learning algorithms can uncover hidden relationships, predict trends, and make accurate forecasts. This enables businesses to fine-tune their strategies, optimize operations, and make data-driven decisions with confidence.

Decision-Making Processes: AI has revolutionized decision-making processes by augmenting human intelligence with automated insights. AI-enabled decision support systems can analyze complex data sets, consider multiple variables, and provide recommendations to aid decision-makers. For instance, in financial services, AI algorithms can analyze market trends, historical data, and risk factors to provide investment recommendations. In healthcare, AI can assist doctors in diagnosing diseases by analyzing patient symptoms, medical records, and research data.

Conclusion:

The integration of AI into industry and business has brought about significant transformations, enhancing productivity, improving customer service, optimizing supply chain management, and enabling data-driven decision-making. However, as AI continues to evolve, it is crucial to address ethical considerations, transparency, and accountability to ensure its responsible and fair usage. As we move forward, AI will undoubtedly continue to shape and redefine industries across the globe, paving the way for a future driven by intelligent automation and innovation.

5 Chapter 5: The Ethical Implications of AI

Introduction: As artificial intelligence (AI) continues to advance at an unprecedented rate, it brings forth an array of ethical concerns that need to be addressed. The potential benefits of AI are vast, but without careful consideration of these ethical implications, we risk undermining its potential and creating unintended consequences. In this chapter, we will explore some of the key ethical concerns related to AI, focusing on bias and fairness in AI algorithms, as well as privacy and security considerations.

Addressing Ethical Concerns Related to AI: As AI becomes increasingly integrated into our daily lives, it is crucial to establish a framework for addressing the ethical concerns that arise. This framework should be built upon transparency, accountability, and a strong understanding of the potential societal impacts. By doing so, we can ensure that AI systems are developed and deployed in a manner that upholds ethical principles and respects human values.

Bias and Fairness in AI Algorithms: One of the most significant ethical concerns surrounding AI is the potential for bias in algorithms. AI algorithms are designed to learn patterns from vast amounts of data, but if that data is biased, the AI system can perpetuate and amplify those biases. This can lead to unfair treatment and discrimination against certain groups, exacerbating existing societal disparities.

To address this concern, it is crucial to ensure diversity and inclusivity in the datasets used to train AI algorithms. Data collection must capture the experiences and perspectives of a

wide range of individuals, representing various demographics, cultures, and backgrounds. Furthermore, AI developers must rigorously test algorithms for bias and fairness throughout the development process. Regular auditing and monitoring of AI systems can help identify and rectify any biases that may emerge over time.

Privacy and Security Considerations: AI systems often require vast amounts of personal data to function effectively. This raises significant concerns regarding privacy and security. Users must have confidence that their personal information will be handled responsibly and protected from unauthorized access or misuse.

To address these concerns, organizations must adopt stringent privacy policies and transparent data handling practices. User consent should be obtained before collecting personal data, and individuals should be provided with clear information about how their data will be used. Additionally, strong safeguards, such as encryption and access controls, should be implemented to protect sensitive data from breaches or unauthorized use.

Furthermore, organizations should prioritize data minimization, ensuring that only the necessary data is collected and stored. Employing techniques like differential privacy can also help protect individual privacy by aggregating and anonymizing data in a way that prevents re-identification.

Conclusion: In this chapter, we have explored the ethical implications, focusing on bias and fairness in AI algorithms, as well as privacy and security considerations. We must address these concerns proactively to ensure the responsible development and deployment of AI systems.

By promoting transparency, accountability, and inclusivity, we can mitigate bias in algorithms and strive for fairness in AI. Moreover, through robust privacy policies, data handling practices, and security measures, we can protect individuals' privacy and maintain their trust in AI technologies. It is incumbent upon AI developers, policymakers, and society as a whole to work collaboratively to navigate these ethical challenges and shape an AI-driven future that benefits all.

6 Chapter 6: The Future of AI

Emerging Trends and Advancements in AI

Artificial Intelligence (AI) has rapidly progressed in recent years, and the future holds even more exciting possibilities. As technology continues to advance, AI is poised to transform various industries and revolutionize the way we live and work. In this chapter, we will explore some of the emerging trends and advancements in AI, along with the potential challenges and opportunities that lie ahead.

One of the most notable trends in AI is the increasing integration of machine learning algorithms into everyday devices and systems. From voice assistants like Siri and Alexa to self-driving cars and smart home automation, AI has become a fundamental part of our daily lives. As computational power and data availability continue to grow, machine learning models are becoming more sophisticated, enabling them to process and analyze massive amounts of information with remarkable accuracy.

Another significant trend is the rapid development of natural language processing (NLP) and natural language generation (NLG) technologies. NLP allows machines to understand and interpret human language, enabling more intuitive interactions between humans and AI systems. This advancement has facilitated the rise of chatbots, language translation tools, and voice recognition systems, making communication seamless and efficient.

Furthermore, AI has made groundbreaking strides in the field of healthcare. With AI-powered diagnostic tools, doctors can analyze medical images, detect anomalies, and provide more accurate diagnoses. AI algorithms can also help predict disease outcomes and personalize treatment plans, revolutionizing patient care. Additionally, AI-enabled robots are assisting surgeries, reducing human error, and improving surgical precision.

In the coming years, autonomous vehicles are expected to become more prevalent. Self-driving cars are equipped with AI systems that can perceive their surroundings, make decisions, and navigate without human intervention. This technology has the potential to reduce accidents, increase transportation efficiency, and transform urban planning. However, challenges related to safety and regulatory frameworks must be addressed before autonomous vehicles can be fully integrated into our society.

Potential Challenges and Opportunities in the Future

As AI evolves, new challenges and opportunities will arise. One significant challenge is the ethical implications of AI. As AI be-

CHAPTER 6: THE FUTURE OF AI

comes more autonomous and capable, questions about privacy, bias, and transparency need to be addressed. Safeguarding data privacy and ensuring fairness in AI algorithms will be crucial to prevent discrimination and protect individual rights.

Another challenge is the potential impact of AI on the job market. While AI automation may eliminate certain jobs, it also has the potential to create new opportunities and enhance human productivity. To mitigate the disruptive effects of AI on employment, continuous re-skilling, and education programs must be developed to equip individuals with the necessary skills for the jobs of the future.

In addition to challenges, the future of AI presents numerous opportunities. AI-driven advancements in personalized medicine, for instance, can significantly improve patient outcomes by tailoring treatments to individual needs. AI can also contribute to addressing global challenges such as climate change, resource management, and sustainable development through optimization models and data-driven decision-making.

Speculations about Artificial General Intelligence (AGI)

Artificial General Intelligence (AGI), often referred to as "strong AI" is the hypothetical development of AI systems that possess human-level intelligence across a wide range of tasks. While current AI systems excel at specific tasks, such as playing chess or diagnosing diseases, they cannot generalize knowledge and skills across domains.

The realization of AGI remains a topic of speculation and debate among experts. Some argue that AGI is an inevitable outcome of AI progress, while others believe that achieving human-level intelligence in machines is an elusive goal. Regardless, the concept of AGI raises important questions about the control, ethics, and impact of highly intelligent machines.

If AGI were to be achieved, it could revolutionize numerous fields such as scientific research, space exploration, and even philosophical inquiry. However, concerns about the potential risks and unintended consequences of AGI must be carefully addressed. Researchers and policymakers must ensure the responsible development and deployment of AGI, prioritizing safety measures, transparency, and robust ethical frameworks.

Conclusion

As the future unfolds, AI has the potential to transform society in ways we can only begin to imagine. Emerging trends and advancements in AI, coupled with the challenges and opportunities they present, provide a glimpse into what lies ahead. While there are uncertainties surrounding AGI, it is clear that AI will continue to evolve, shaping our world and offering immense possibilities for progress and innovation.

7 Chapter 7: AI and Society

Societal impacts of AI adoption, job displacement, and workforce transformation, as well as promoting responsible and inclusive AI development, are crucial aspects that demand careful consideration in today's rapidly evolving technological landscape. As artificial intelligence (AI) becomes increasingly integrated into our lives, it is vital to understand both the benefits and challenges it presents to society. This chapter delves into these topics, exploring the potential consequences and proposing strategies for a more responsible and inclusive future.

The widespread adoption of AI brings with it significant societal impacts. On the positive side, AI has the potential to revolutionize various sectors, from healthcare to transportation, by improving efficiency, accuracy, and decision-making processes. AI-powered technologies can save lives through early disease detection, enable safer transportation through autonomous vehicles, and enhance customer experiences through personalized recommendations. However, we must also acknowledge the challenges that come with AI adoption.

Job displacement is a chief concern surrounding AI. As AI technologies automate tasks previously performed by humans, certain jobs become obsolete or require a different skill set. This disruption can lead to unemployment and economic inequality if proper measures are not in place. To mitigate these effects, it is crucial to focus on workforce transformation. Governments, educational institutions, and organizations must collaborate to provide -opportunities that seek risk. By investing in lifelong learning programs and fostering a culture of continuous education, we can ensure that workers are equipped with the skills needed to thrive in an AI-driven economy.

Moreover, promoting responsible and inclusive AI development is vital to prevent the exacerbation of existing societal biases and inequities. AI systems learn from data, and if the training data is biased or incomplete, the resulting algorithms can perpetuate discrimination or reinforce social inequalities. To address this, data collection and curation processes must be transparent, diverse, and representative of the populations they serve. It is essential to engage a multidisciplinary group of experts, including ethicists, sociologists, and social scientists, in the development and deployment of AI systems. By incorporating diverse perspectives, we can actively work towards minimizing bias and ensuring fairness and inclusivity in AI technologies.

To further promote responsible AI development, frameworks and guidelines are necessary. Governments and regulatory bodies should collaborate with industry leaders to develop

CHAPTER 7: AI AND SOCIETY

ethically sound and legally enforceable standards. These frameworks should encompass aspects such as privacy, security, transparency, and accountability in AI systems. By establishing a robust regulatory environment, we can foster trust in AI technologies and protect individuals' rights, ensuring that AI is used for the betterment of society while minimizing potential harm.

Collaborative efforts between academia, industry, and civil society are crucial for addressing the societal impacts of AI adoption. Public-private partnerships can facilitate the sharing of knowledge, expertise, and resources. These collaborations can foster innovation while ensuring that AI development aligns
with societal values and serves the collective good. Additionally, open dialogue and engagement with the public are essential to build trust and transparency in AI systems. Regular forums, public consultations, and education campaigns can facilitate understanding and awareness among individuals, allowing them to actively participate in shaping AI's role in society.

In conclusion, the societal impacts of AI adoption are wide-ranging and require careful consideration. While AI holds immense potential, it also poses challenges such as job displacement and biased algorithms. By prioritizing workforce transformation initiatives, promoting responsible AI development, and fostering collaboration between various stakeholders, we can navigate these challenges and build a more inclusive and equitable future. As AI continues to evolve, we must shape its development in a way that maximizes societal benefits while ensuring fairness, accountability, and respect for human rights. By doing so, we can harness the transformative power of AI to create a better world for all.

8 Chapter 8: AI in Education

Introduction

Artificial Intelligence (AI) has emerged as a transformative force across various industries, and education is no exception. Integrating AI into educational tools and platforms has the potential to revolutionize the way students learn and teachers instruct. This chapter explores the integration of AI in educational tools and platforms, personalized learning experiences facilitated by AI algorithms, and the ethical considerations and challenges that arise in AI-powered education.

Integration of AI in Educational Tools and Platforms

The integration of AI in educational tools and platforms holds immense promise for enhancing the quality and effectiveness of education. AI algorithms can analyze vast amounts of educational data, including student performance, learning patterns, and educational resources, enabling the development of intelligent tools that adapt to individual student needs. These tools can provide personalized feedback, recommend tailored learning resources, and even predict future learning outcomes.

One prominent example of AI integration is the use of intelligent tutoring systems. These systems leverage AI algorithms to provide personalized learning experiences, acting as virtual tutors that adapt to individual learner requirements. By analyzing student performance, these systems identify knowledge gaps and deliver targeted instruction. Moreover, they provide real-time feedback, fostering a more interactive and engaging learning environment.

AI-powered assessment tools also offer significant benefits. These tools leverage natural language processing and machine learning techniques to automatically evaluate and provide feedback on student assignments and exams. By automating these processes, teachers can save time and focus on providing more personalized instruction.

Personalized Learning Experiences Using AI Algorithms

AI algorithms enable the delivery of personalized learning experiences that cater to individual student needs, abilities, and interests. Personalized learning harnesses AI's potential to adapt instructional content, pace, and delivery methods to maximize student engagement and achievement.

Through AI-powered adaptive learning platforms, students can access customized learning materials, exercises, and assessments. These platforms analyze a student's performance and learning behavior to create personalized learning paths. By

identifying areas of strength and weakness, adaptive learning systems provide tailored content and recommendations, supporting students in their unique learning journeys.

Furthermore, AI can facilitate differentiated instruction, ensuring that each student receives appropriate learning content and challenges. Machine learning algorithms can analyze extensive educational data to classify students into different proficiency levels and suggest appropriate learning resources, ensuring optimal learning outcomes for all.

Ethical Considerations and Challenges in AI-powered Education

While AI-powered education offers immense potential, it also presents ethical considerations and challenges that must be addressed. One primary concern is data privacy and security. AI systems collect and process vast amounts of student data, including personal information and performance records. It is crucial to establish robust data protection measures and ensure that data is used responsibly and ethically, safeguarding students' privacy.

Another challenge lies in the potential bias embedded in AI algorithms. Machine learning algorithms learn from historical data, which may contain biases that perpetuate discrimination or reinforce existing inequalities in education. Proper data cleaning and algorithmic auditing are essential to ensure fairness and equity in AI-powered educational tools and platforms.

Furthermore, the reliance on AI systems should not replace human teachers but rather complement their expertise. While AI tools can enhance instruction and provide personalized learning experiences, the human element in education, such as mentorship, emotional support, and critical thinking, remains vital.

Conclusion

Chapter 8 explored the integration of AI in educational tools and platforms, highlighting the potential for personalized learning experiences and the ethical considerations and challenges in AI-powered education. The transformative capabilities of AI offer exciting possibilities for enhancing education, but it is crucial to address ethical concerns and ensure that AI remains a tool to support and empower educators and students rather than replace them.

9 Chapter 9: AI and Environmental Sustainability

Introduction

As the world grapples with the urgent need for environmental conservation and sustainable practices, the potential of artificial intelligence(AI) to address these issues has become increasingly significant. AI offers immense opportunities for monitoring, conservation efforts, sustainable agriculture, and resource management. However, it is important to acknowledge and address the potential carbon footprint associated with AI technologies. In this chapter, we will explore how AI can contribute to environmental sustainability and discuss strategies to mitigate its impact on the environment.

Utilizing AI for Environmental Monitoring and Conservation Efforts

One of the most promising applications of AI lies in its ability to enhance environmental monitoring and conservation efforts.

AI can process vast amounts of data collected from satellites, sensors, and other sources, enabling more accurate and timely environmental assessments. For example, AI-powered image recognition algorithms can analyze satellite imagery to identify changes in land cover, deforestation, or illegal logging activities. This enables authorities to respond swiftly, mitigating the damage and enforcing regulations.

Furthermore, AI algorithms can process acoustic data to identify species and patterns in animal vocalizations, aiding in wildlife conservation. By analyzing large datasets, AI can automatically detect and classify biodiversity hotspots, helping researchers and conservationists prioritize their efforts.

Applications of AI in Sustainable Agriculture and Resource Management

Another critical area where AI can contribute to environmental sustainability is in agriculture and resource management. By leveraging AI, farmers can optimize resource usage, reduce waste, and increase yields. AI algorithms can analyze soil conditions, crop health, and weather patterns to recommend precise amounts of irrigation, fertilizers, and pesticides, minimizing the impact on the environment. This not only promotes sustainable agricultural practices but also reduces the amount of harmful chemicals released into ecosystems.

AI can also play a vital role in resource management. Machine learning algorithms can analyze historical and real-time data on energy consumption, water usage patterns, and waste generation to identify opportunities for efficiency improvements. For

CHAPTER 9: AI AND ENVIRONMENTAL SUSTAINABILITY

instance, AI can optimize power generation and distribution, reducing energy losses and carbon emissions. Similarly, AI-powered systems can monitor and optimize water usage in industrial processes, minimizing wastage and preserving this precious resource.

Addressing the Carbon Footprint of AI Technologies

While AI presents immense potential for environmental sustainability, it is crucial to address the carbon footprint associated with these technologies.

AI models, particularly those requiring significant computational power, can consume substantial amounts of energy, leading to increased greenhouse gas emissions.

To mitigate this impact, several approaches can be adopted. First, there is a need for continued research and development in energy-efficient AI algorithms and hardware. Innovations such as low-power AI chips and algorithms that require fewer computational resources can significantly reduce the energy consumption of AI systems.

Secondly, renewable energy sources should power AI infrastructure whenever possible. By shifting to renewable energy, we can minimize the carbon emissions associated with AI technologies. Governments, organizations, and AI developers should prioritize sourcing their energy needs from renewable sources and invest in the development of renewable energy infrastructure.

Lastly, responsible AI usage is fundamental. Organizations should adopt policies and practices that promote efficiency, including optimizing algorithms to reduce computational requirements and avoiding unnecessary duplication of AI systems. Additionally, the responsible disposal and recycling of AI hardware should be prioritized to minimize electronic waste.

Conclusion

In this chapter, we have explored the potential of AI to contribute to environmental sustainability through monitoring, conservation efforts, sustainable agriculture, and resource management. While AI offers immense promise, it is crucial to address the associated carbon footprint. By advancing energy-efficient algorithms, utilizing renewable energy sources, and promoting responsible AI usage, we can harness the power of AI while minimizing its impact on the environment. The next chapter will delve into the ethical considerations surrounding AI and its implications for society.

10 Chapter 10: AI in Governance and Public Policy

Introduction

Artificial Intelligence (AI) has permeated various sectors, revolutionizing the way tasks are performed and systems are managed. In governance and public policy, AI has the potential to enhance service delivery, streamline decision-making processes, and improve overall efficiency. However, the implementation of AI in these domains comes with a myriad of ethical, legal, and accountability challenges. This chapter explores the critical aspects of implementing AI in public service delivery and governance, the ethical and legal considerations in AI-driven policymaking, as well as the importance of transparency and accountability in AI-powered governmental systems.

Implementing AI in Public Service Delivery and Governance

The integration of AI technologies in public service delivery has the potential to optimize processes, enhance citizen experience, and reduce costs. AI-powered chatbots, for instance, can provide automated responses to citizen queries, offer personalized recommendations, and handle routine administrative tasks. This not only frees up human resources but also ensures citizens receive timely and accurate information. Additionally, AI algorithms can analyze vast amounts of data to identify patterns, trends, and anomalies, allowing policymakers to make informed decisions based on evidence.

Governance itself stands to benefit from AI implementation. AI can aid in identifying potential vulnerabilities in critical infrastructure, predicting disease outbreaks, optimizing transportation networks, and even forecasting economic trends. By harnessing the power of machine learning and predictive analytics, governments can anticipate risks, allocate resources efficiently, and devise effective policies to address emerging challenges.

Ethical and Legal Considerations in AI-Driven Policymaking

While AI presents numerous opportunities, its adoption in policymaking raises ethical and legal concerns. Policymakers must ensure that AI systems operate in a manner that aligns with societal values and principles. Ethical considerations include fairness, accountability, transparency, and privacy. It is essential to avoid biased decision-making by ensuring that AI algorithms are trained on diverse datasets that accurately represent the population. Policymakers must also establish mechanisms to address the potential for unintended consequences, such as job displacement due to automation.

Legal considerations involve compliance with existing regulations and the development of new legislation tailored to AI applications. Policymakers must navigate issues related to data protection, intellectual property rights, liability, and accountability. They should establish legal frameworks that hold AI developers and users accountable for any harm caused by AI systems. Additionally, privacy concerns must be addressed to safeguard citizen data and prevent misuse.

Transparency and Accountability in AI-Powered Governmental Systems

Transparency and accountability are paramount when it comes to AI-driven governmental systems. Citizens must have confidence in the decisions made by AI systems and understand the logic and reasoning behind them. To achieve this, policymakers should ensure the transparency of AI algorithms and foster explainability. AI systems should be designed in a way that allows for clear audits and assessments to identify biases, errors, or discriminatory outcomes.

Accountability mechanisms should be established to hold both AI systems and human users accountable for their actions. Policymakers must define responsibility and liability frameworks to address potential harms caused by AI systems, ensuring that individuals and organizations are held accountable for any negative consequences resulting from their use. Furthermore, governments should proactively engage with stakeholders to foster public trust and ensure that the deployment of AI aligns with societal values.

Conclusion

The integration of AI in governance and public policy has the potential to deliver significant improvements, ranging from enhanced service delivery to optimized decision-making processes. However, the implementation of AI should be accompanied by careful consideration of ethical and legal implications, ensuring fairness, accountability, and transparency. Transparency is crucial to build public trust, while accountability mechanisms guarantee the responsible use of AI systems. By effectively addressing these challenges, policymakers can harness the transformative power of AI to build a better future for citizens and drive inclusive governance and policy-making.

11 Chapter 11: AI and Creativity

Introduction

In recent years, the rapid advancements in Artificial Intelligence
(AI) have sparked debates and discussions about its potential impact on
creativity. While creativity has historically been considered a purely human
attribute, the emergence of AI technologies has opened new doors for
exploration and collaboration in creative industries such as art, music, and
literature. This chapter delves into the role of AI in these industries, the
collaborative possibilities between AI and human creators, and the
challenges and controversies surrounding AI-generated content.

Exploring AI's Role in Creative Industries

The infusion of AI into creative industries has brought about both excitement
and skepticism. AI has demonstrated its ability to generate artwork, compose
music, and even write literature. In the realm of art, AI algorithms can analyze
vast amounts of data to produce thought-provoking visual pieces.
Organizations like Google's Deep Dream have used AI to create surreal and
intriguing images by training neural networks to identify patterns and
reimagine them in innovative ways.

Similarly, AI's impact on the music industry has been notable. AI algorithms
can analyze vast musical databases, recognize patterns, and generate new
compositions that mimic the styles of renowned musicians. Projects like Juke
Deck and Amper have leveraged AI to create original, royalty-free music for

videos and advertisements, reducing the need for expensive licensing or custom compositions.

In the domain of literature, AI has even ventured into writing poetry and short stories. AI models, such as OpenAI's GPT3, have learned to generate coherent and engaging text that closely resembles human-written content. This breakthrough has sparked discussions about the potential democratization of storytelling, as AI could assist writers by generating ideas or even co-authoring.

Collaborative Possibilities Between AI and Human Creators

Rather than replacing human creativity, AI has the potential to augment and collaborate with human creators, opening up new avenues for innovation. The combination of human imagination and AI's computational power offers a unique synergy that can lead to remarkable outcomes.

In the art world, many artists have started utilizing AI as a tool in their creative process, leveraging its ability to generate

CHAPTER 11: AI AND CREATIVITY

alternative ideas and explore uncharted territories. Artists like Mario Klingemann have embraced AI, using it as a medium to produce provocative artworks that challenge traditional notions of creativity. AI-driven tools, such as Style GAN, allow artists to create hyper-realistic images that blend multiple artistic styles, breathing new life into traditional art forms.

Music creators, too, have embraced AI as a partner in their creative journey. Rather than seeing AI as a threat, artists like Taryn Southern have used AI algorithms to generate melodies or find harmonies that inspire their compositions. This collaborative approach has opened doors to experimentation, enabling musicians to push the boundaries of their creativity and explore unexplored sonic landscapes.

In literature, AI has shown promise in assisting writers with generating ideas, enhancing productivity, and even co-authoring. Writers can leverage AI models to overcome writer's block, explore alternative storylines, or develop characters with unique perspectives. By working together with AI, creators can tap into the vast knowledge and creativity embedded in AI algorithms, complementing their abilities and expanding the realm of storytelling possibilities.

Challenges and Controversies Surrounding AI-Generated Content

While the integration of AI into creative industries presents exciting opportunities, it also raises significant challenges and controversies. One pressing concern is the attribution of AI-generated content. As AI models become more sophisticated, it becomes increasingly difficult to discern whether a piece of art, music, or literature has been solely created by a human or generated with AI assistance. This raises questions about copyright, intellectual property, and the ethical implications of AI's creative contributions.

Moreover, AI-generated content has also been criticized for lacking the depth of human emotion and subjective experiences. Critics argue that AI algorithms lack a genuine understanding of human emotions and cultural context, resulting in pieces that may appear technically proficient but lack the inherent human touch that resonates with audiences. The debate surrounding the authenticity and emotional impact of AI-generated content continues to be a topic of contention in creative circles.

Conclusion

Chapter 11 has explored the role of AI in creative industries, highlighting its potential impact on art, music, and literature. AI has demonstrated its ability to generate content, leading to collaborative possibilities between AI and human creators. However, challenges and controversies surrounding AI-generated content, such as attribution and authenticity, remain at the forefront of discussions. As the relationship between AI and creativity evolves, it is crucial to navigate these complexities to ensure that AI becomes a powerful tool that enriches, rather than diminishes, human creativity.

12 Chapter 12: AI and Healthcare Transformation

Introduction: Artificial Intelligence (AI) has emerged as a groundbreaking technology that holds immense potential for transforming the healthcare industry. In this chapter, we will explore how AI is revolutionizing healthcare delivery through its ability to enable diagnostics and treatment. Additionally, we will delve into the ethical considerations surrounding AI-driven healthcare decision-making.

Revolutionizing Healthcare Delivery through AI-enabled Diagnostics and Treatment:

Enhanced Diagnostic Accuracy: AI has demonstrated remarkable capabilities in analyzing medical imaging, such as X-rays, MRIs, and CT scans, leading to improved diagnostic accuracy. Machine learning algorithms can quickly and accurately identify potential abnormalities, enabling healthcare professionals to make more informed decisions. This ability to detect and diagnose diseases at an early stage enhances the chances of successful treatment and reduces the risk of misdiagnosis.

Predictive Analytics: AI algorithms can process vast amounts of patient data, including medical records, family history, and lifestyle factors, to predict disease outcomes and identify high-risk patients. By analyzing patterns and trends within these datasets, AI can assist healthcare providers in developing personalized treatment plans, preventive interventions, and early intervention strategies.

Precision Medicine: The integration of AI with genomics has catalyzed the field of precision medicine. By examining a patient's genetic profile, AI algorithms can predict their response to certain medications, identify potential drug interactions, and guide healthcare professionals in selecting the most effective therapies. This personalized approach minimizes adverse reactions, optimizes treatment outcomes, and empowers patients with tailored healthcare solutions.

Robotic Surgery and Assistance: AI-powered robots are revolutionizing the field of surgery. With enhanced precision, stability, and dexterity, surgical robots can perform complex procedures with minimal invasiveness, reducing recovery times and improving patient outcomes. Furthermore, AI-enabled robotic assistance aids surgeons during complex surgeries by providing real-time feedback, enhancing accuracy, and reducing the risk of errors.

Ethical Considerations in AI-driven Healthcare Decisionmaking:

Privacy and Data Security: The use of AI in healthcare requires access to vast amounts of patient data. Ensuring the privacy and security of this data is paramount to maintaining patient trust. Healthcare organizations must establish robust protocols to protect patient information, including encryption, secure storage, and strict access controls. Transparent consent and data-sharing policies are essential to build a foundation of trust between patients, healthcare providers, and AI systems.

Bias and Fairness: AI algorithms can inadvertently perpetuate biases present in the data they are trained on, leading to unequal access to healthcare services and unequal treatment outcomes. It is crucial to address these biases by continuously monitoring and updating algorithms, diversifying training datasets, and involving multidisciplinary teams to ensure fairness in decision-making processes.

Accountability and Liability: As AI systems become increasingly integrated into healthcare decision-making, questions arise regarding accountability and liability. In cases of adverse outcomes or errors, determining responsibility between human operators and AI systems can be challenging. Healthcare organizations must establish clear frameworks for accountability, ensuring that human oversight remains an integral part of AI-driven healthcare processes.

Transparency and Explainability: AI algorithms often operate as "black boxes," making it difficult to understand the reasoning behind their decisions. In healthcare, explainability is crucial to ensure trust and facilitate informed decision-making. Researchers must strive to develop AI systems that provide explanations for their decisions, enabling healthcare providers to understand and validate the recommendations made by AI algorithms.

Conclusion: AI has the potential to revolutionize healthcare delivery by improving diagnostic accuracy, enabling personalized medicine, and enhancing surgical procedures. However, along with these advancements, ethical considerations must be addressed to ensure patient privacy, fairness, and accountability. By embracing AI while maintaining human oversight and ethical frameworks, we can harness its transformative power to make healthcare more accessible, accurate, and patient-centered.

13 Chapter 13: AI and Cybersecurity

Introduction

In recent years, the field of cybersecurity has witnessed a significant increase in the sophistication and frequency of cyber threats. As technology evolves, cybercriminals continue to exploit vulnerabilities in our digital systems, putting individuals, organizations, and governments at risk. To counter these threats, the integration of Artificial Intelligence (AI) has emerged as a powerful tool for detecting and preventing cyberattacks. This chapter will explore the role of AI in cybersecurity, specifically focusing on how it detects and prevents cyber threats through machine learning, while also addressing the ethical considerations surrounding its use for privacy protection. The Role of AI in Detecting and Preventing Cyber Threats

AI is revolutionizing the cybersecurity landscape by enhancing threat detection and prevention mechanisms. Traditional security methods primarily rely on signature-based approaches, which can only detect known threats. However, with the rapid evolution of malicious techniques, these methods are becoming less effective. AI, on the other hand, employs advanced algorithms and deep learning models to detect anomalies and patterns that may indicate malicious activities.

Leveraging Machine Learning for Anomaly Detection and Pattern Recognition

One of the significant contributions of AI in cybersecurity is its ability to leverage machine learning techniques for anomaly detection and pattern recognition. Machine learning algorithms can analyze vast amounts of data to identify anomalies that deviate from normal behavior. By establishing baselines and learning from historical data, AI systems can identify deviations that may indicate the presence of a cyber threat.

Moreover, AI can recognize patterns in data that may not be evident to human analysts. This capability allows for the early detection of threats, allowing organizations to respond proactively before significant damage occurs. Furthermore, AI systems can continuously learn and adapt, evolving alongside emerging cyber threats, making them indispensable in the fight against cybercrime.

Ethical Considerations in the Use of AI for Cybersecurity and Privacy Protection

While AI presents immense potential in enhancing cybersecurity measures, its implementation must be accompanied by strong ethical considerations. Privacy protection is a critical concern,

CHAPTER 13: AI AND CYBERSECURITY

as AI systems require access to vast amounts of data to learn and detect threats effectively. Organizations must ensure that the collection and processing of data align with legal frameworks and respect individuals' privacy rights.

Transparency in AI algorithms is another ethical consideration. Organizations must strive to provide clear explanations of how their systems make decisions, particularly when it comes to the identification of potential threats. This transparency fosters trust and allows individuals and organizations to understand and assess the reliability of AI-driven cybersecurity systems.

Bias within AI systems is also an important ethical concern. As
AI algorithms are trained on historical data, they may inherit biases present
in the data itself. These biases can result in discriminatory practices, which
have severe consequences, particularly in the context of cybersecurity.
Organizations must actively work towards ensuring fairness and
accountability in AI algorithms, regularly auditing and evaluating their
systems for potential bias.

Conclusion

In an era where cyber threats continue to escalate, the role of
AI in cybersecurity is pivotal. Its ability to detect and prevent cyber-attacks
through machine learning techniques, anomaly detection, and pattern
recognition empowers organizations to stay one step ahead of
cybercriminals. However, as AI becomes more integrated into cybersecurity
practices, ethical considerations regarding privacy protection, transparency,
and bias must be addressed. By upholding these ethical principles,
organizations can harness the power of AI to safeguard our digital
environment while ensuring fairness, accountability, and respect for
individual privacy.

14 Chapter 14: AI and Human-Computer Interaction

Introduction

In recent years, the rapid advancement of Artificial Intelligence (AI) has revolutionized the way humans interact with computers. From voice assistants to chatbots, AI-powered interfaces have significantly enhanced user experiences, making technology more intuitive, personalized, and accessible. This chapter explores the various aspects of AI and Human-Computer Interaction (HCI), focusing on enhancing user experience, the emergence of voice assistants and chatbots, and the importance of designing inclusive and user-friendly AI systems.

Enhancing User Experience through AI-powered Interfaces and Interactions

AI-powered interfaces have redefined user experience by leveraging machine learning and cognitive technologies to understand and predict user preferences. These interfaces can adapt to users' behaviors and provide personalized recommendations, thus streamlining the interaction process. By analyzing vast amounts of data, AI systems can identify patterns and trends, enabling them to make accurate predictions about user needs and optimize their experiences.

For instance, online marketplaces employ AI algorithms to analyze past purchases, browsing history, and customer preferences, enhancing the overall shopping experience. AI-powered interfaces also improve search engines by understanding user intent and returning more relevant results.

Moreover, AI has transformed user interactions by enabling natural language processing and computer vision. Voice assistants like Siri, Alexa, and Google Assistant have become integral parts of our daily lives, allowing users to interact with technology through voice commands. These assistants are designed to understand the context and respond to inquiries, perform tasks, and provide relevant information. Through AI, voice assistants have become intuitive and conversational, making technology more accessible and user-friendly.

Chatbots, another AI-driven interface, have also gained popularity across various industries. These virtual assistants engage in automated conversations with users, providing instant customer support, answering queries, and even performing transactions. Chatbots are particularly useful in industries such as e-commerce, healthcare, and banking, where they can handle routine inquiries, freeing human agents to focus on complex issues. Through AI, chatbots offer round-the-clock

assistance, ensuring prompt responses and improved customer satisfaction.

Designing Inclusive and User-Friendly AI Systems

As AI becomes more prevalent, it is crucial to ensure that AI systems are designed to be inclusive and user-friendly, catering to the diverse needs and abilities of all users. Designers must consider various factors, such as accessibility, transparency, and ethical implications, to create AI systems that promote inclusivity and enhance the user experience.

When designing AI interfaces, it is essential to consider accessibility for users with disabilities. For visually impaired users, AI systems can provide text-to-speech or braille outputs, enabling them to interact effectively. Similarly, speech recognition technology allows users with limited mobility to interact with AI systems effortlessly. Designers must prioritize universal design principles to ensure that AI interfaces are accessible to all individuals, regardless of their abilities.

Transparency and explainability are critical for building trust in AI systems. Users should have a clear understanding of how AI interfaces work and the data they collect. By providing explanations for AI-driven decisions and being transparent about data usage, designers can foster user trust and mitigate concerns related to privacy and security.

Moreover, ethical considerations in AI design are paramount. AI systems should adhere to ethical guidelines, avoiding biases and discrimination. Designers must ensure that AI interfaces are fair, transparent, and accountable. Regular audits and evaluations can help identify and rectify any biases or unintended consequences that may arise from the use of AI systems.

Conclusion

Chapter 14 explores the impact of AI on Human-Computer Interaction, focusing on enhancing user experience, the emergence of voice assistants and chatbots, and the importance of designing inclusive and user-friendly AI systems. AI-powered interfaces have transformed user experiences by personalizing interactions, adapting to user behavior, and providing tailored recommendations. Voice assistants and chatbots have made technology more accessible and intuitive, enabling natural language interactions and automated conversations. However, as AI continues to evolve, it is essential to design AI systems that prioritize inclusivity, transparency, and ethical considerations. By doing so, we can harness the full potential of AI to enhance human-computer interactions while ensuring a user-friendly and inclusive digital future.

15 Chapter 15: AI and Urban Planning

Introduction: In recent years, the rapid advancements in artificial intelligence (AI) have opened up new possibilities for urban planning and management. This chapter explores the diverse applications of AI in smart city development, predictive analytics for traffic management and infrastructure planning, as well as the importance of addressing societal concerns such as privacy and surveillance in AI-powered urban environments.

Utilizing A I for Smart City Development and Urban Management: AI technologies provide an unprecedented opportunity to create smarter, more efficient, and sustainable cities. By leveraging the power of AI-driven algorithms, urban planners can make better decisions in areas such as transportation, energy, waste management, and public safety.

One key application of AI in smart city development is the integration of various data streams to optimize urban functions. For instance, AI algorithms can analyze real-time data from sensors, satellite imagery, and social media feeds to gain insights into urban patterns and trends. This information can then be used to improve mobility, optimize energy consumption, and enhance the overall quality of life for citizens.

Predictive Analytics for Traffic Management and Infrastructure Planning: AI-powered predictive analytics has become a game-changer in traffic management and infrastructure planning. By analyzing vast amounts of historical and real-time data, AI algorithms can accurately forecast traffic patterns, identify congestion hotspots, and recommend optimal routes for commuters.

Furthermore, AI can assist in infrastructure planning by simulating scenarios and predicting the impact of proposed changes. For example, urban planners can use AI to simulate the effects of building new roads, bridges, or public transportation systems. By considering factors like population growth, demographic shifts, and economic trends, AI can help identify the most cost-effective and efficient infrastructure solutions.

Addressing Societal Concerns: While AI offers tremendous potential in urban planning, it also raises important societal concerns that must be addressed. Privacy and surveillance are two critical issues that need careful attention in AI-powered urban environments.

As AI systems process vast amounts of personal data, concerns arise regarding how this data is collected, stored, and used. Governments and city authorities must ensure that comprehensive privacy regulations are in place to protect citizens' personal information. Additionally, transparency and accountability in

CHAPTER 15: AI AND URBAN PLANNING

AI algorithms are crucial to building trust among citizens. Regular audits and third-party assessments of AI systems can help ensure that they are free from bias and discrimination.

Surveillance is another concern in AI-powered urban environments. AI can be used to monitor public spaces, analyze video feeds for security purposes, and detect potentially criminal activities. However, it is essential to strike a balance between ensuring public safety and preserving individual privacy. Clear regulations and guidelines should be established to define the boundaries of surveillance, preventing potential abuse or violation of citizens' rights.

Conclusion: Chapter 15 has explored the immense potential of AI in urban planning and management. Through the utilization of AI for smart city development, predictive analytics for traffic management and infrastructure planning, and addressing societal concerns such as privacy and surveillance, cities can harness the power of AI to create more efficient, sustainable, and livable urban environments. However, cities must navigate these developments with a clear focus on privacy, transparency, and accountability to ensure that AI is utilized responsibly for the benefit of all citizens.

16 Chapter 16: AI in Space Exploration

Introduction

The exploration of space has always been a captivating endeavor, pushing the boundaries of human knowledge and understanding. Over the years, the quest for discovery has seen remarkable advancements, and the integration of artificial intelligence (AI) has played a pivotal role in revolutionizing space exploration. In this chapter, we will delve into the applications of AI in space missions, satellite operations, and planetary exploration. We will explore the impact of autonomous spacecraft navigation and decision-making, as well as the collaborative efforts between AI and human astronauts for deep space exploration.

Applications of AI in Space Missions, Satellite Operations, and Planetary Exploration

AI has proven to be a game-changer in various aspects of space missions. One of its primary applications is in satellite operations, where AI systems assist in managing vast arrays of

satellites. These intelligent systems monitor satellite health, predict malfunctions, and optimize their performance. By analyzing copious amounts of data, AI can identify patterns and anomalies that humans may miss, ensuring the smooth functioning of satellites and reducing the risk of failures.

Furthermore, AI plays a crucial role in planetary exploration. Robotic rovers, such as NASA's Curiosity on Mars, rely on AI to autonomously navigate and make decisions in real-time. These rovers are equipped with computer vision systems that allow them to analyze their surroundings, identify geological features, and plan their movements accordingly. By leveraging AI, these rovers can adapt to unforeseen obstacles, execute complex maneuvers, and carry out scientific experiments with reduced human intervention.

Autonomous Spacecraft Navigation and Decision-Making

In addition to planetary rovers, AI has enabled autonomous spacecraft navigation, enhancing our ability to explore the vastness of space. Traditionally, spacecraft navigation required continuous communication with ground control, leading to delays and limitations in exploration. However, AI-powered autonomous navigation systems have transformed this scenario.

These systems use machine learning algorithms to process vast amounts of data, including telemetry, sensor readings, and celestial observations. By analyzing this data in real-time, AI systems can accurately determine the spacecraft's position, velocity, and orientation. This enables autonomous navigation, freeing space missions from the limitations of ground control

and allowing for more efficient exploration of distant celestial bodies.

Moreover, AI empowers spacecraft to make intelligent decisions in response to expected events. With the ability to analyze and process data rapidly, AI systems can identify potential hazards and adjust course or mission objectives accordingly. This capability becomes increasingly critical during long-duration space missions, where the time delay in communication renders human decision-making impractical. The integration of AI ensures that spacecraft can autonomously respond to dynamic conditions, enhancing safety and expanding the scope of exploration.

Collaborative Efforts between AI and Human Astronauts for Deep Space Exploration

While AI has brought significant advancements to space exploration, human astronauts remain indispensable for certain missions. Deep space exploration, in particular, requires the collaboration between AI systems and human astronauts to overcome the challenges posed by vast distances and extended durations.

AI systems can assist astronauts in numerous ways during deep space missions. They can analyze and process data from onboard sensors, providing real-time insights and alerts. This aids astronauts in making informed decisions, optimizing resource utilization, and increasing mission efficiency. Additionally, AI systems can help monitor the health and well-being of astronauts, detecting anomalies or potential health issues before they

CHAPTER 16: AI IN SPACE EXPLORATION

become critical.

Furthermore, AI systems can enhance the effectiveness of scientific experiments conducted by astronauts. By leveraging machine learning algorithms, these systems can analyze vast amounts of data collected during experiments, identifying patterns and correlations that human scientists may miss. Such capabilities enable astronauts to carry out more comprehensive research and maximize the scientific output of their missions.

Conclusion

The integration of AI in space exploration has opened up new frontiers and expanded our understanding of the universe. From satellite operations to planetary exploration, AI has proven invaluable in enhancing mission success rates and reducing human intervention. The advent of autonomous spacecraft navigation and decision-making has enabled deeper space exploration while ensuring the safety and efficiency of missions. Moreover, collaborative efforts between AI systems and human astronauts have facilitated complex deep space exploration missions, augmenting the capabilities of both man and machine.

As we continue to unlock the secrets of the cosmos, the partnership between AI and human explorers will undoubtedly play a pivotal role in shaping the future of space exploration.

17 Chapter 17

www.ingramcontent.com/pod-product-compliance
Lightning Source LLC
LaVergne TN
LVHW051619050326
832903LV00033B/4576